Simply
Inspirational
Writing

SIMPLY INSPIRATIONAL WRITING

From the influence of White
Feather through the mediumship
of Karen North

Karen North

To order additional copies of this book, contact:
Xlibris Corporation
0-800-644-6988
www.xlibrispublishing.co.uk
Orders@xlibrispublishing.co.uk
301974

Contents

PEACE

Our Father, we send out our thoughts to promote peace within our World.

P   Signifies purity, a Divine Force which will penetrate hatred into Love.

E   Is for everyone to participate, whatever caste or creed, to join together and prove their love towards mankind.

A   The awareness of truth, which must be passed on to others, and leads to—

C   The Christ consciousness within, to unfold and enrich man's understanding.

E   Is Everlasting, knowing that peace shall never be destroyed through man's own folly.

We ask that the peace felt within our hearts, will be given to those in need, through thy name of Love.

Amen.

10th November, 1986

A WHITE ROSE

White represents the spirit which should be glowing bright
Many search to find the key of life
That will unlock the door to eternity
The path undoubtedly will be one of strife
And it must be undertaken in truth and light

The Rose represents a sturdy, but very delicate flower
So tend to your thoughts as a garden
To enable the knowledge to blossom forth
Then truth withstands the thorns and will pardon
To reveal that spirit is Love—the Divine power.

5th January, 1987

OBEDIENCE

O   Is Omnipotent the Infinite power, the God-head.

B   Is Birth the awakening, the beginning.

E   Is Everlasting for the spiritual life is continuous.

D   Is the Divine spark the light within.

I   Is Intuition which must be acknowledged.

E   Is Encouragement to follow the light.

N   Is for Nature the essence of life to be understood.

C   Is for Compliance as you sow, so shall you reap.

E   Is for escape—there is no escape, life must be fulfilled.

7th January, 1987

COMMUNION

C   Is Contentment in knowing the truth of life.

O   Onward, the direction in which to travel the path.

M   Master of your own destiny towards the light.

M   Is for Maturity, which is needed in the understanding of the knowledge gained.

U   Union, of the mind, body and soul, perfection, to be strived for.

N   Signifies the Naturalness, with which your spiritual gifts will unfold.

I   Inspiration, the source from which you will blossom and grow.

O   Open the channel, in order to receive, and then it must be passed on to those ready to listen.

N   Is for the News, to be announced to the World, that PEACE is the prize.

19th January, 1987

ILLUMINOUS

I   Is for Illustration of the perfect way of life as demonstrated by the Son of God.

L   Is for Love, the gift of God, given to mankind.

L   Is for Light, the manifestation of Love.

U   Is for Unity of thought, to enable the Light to grow within.

M   Is for the Mountains you will have to climb in search of the truth.

I   Is Instinct, your inner-self to be followed in your quest.

N   Is for the Negative forces which exist to try to extinguish to Light.

O   Is for Outstanding, as your achievements will be great, when you acquire ....

U   Understanding of your part to play, when your inner-light will ....

S   Shine, into the darkness of the World, bringing happiness, peace and tranquillity to those you meet.

21st January, 1987

MINISTRY

M   Meditation is the key that will free your spirit.

I   Individuality, you must understand yourself, before you can comprehend the truth of life.

N   Nearness of spirit, the life that stirs within, to be felt most distinctly.

I   Indebtedness, to the Love of God, that enables the light to go forth in . . . .

S   Service to others, remembering to do unto others as you would have done unto you, and then . . .

T   Trust in the Love, which is so freely given, and use all of the . . . .

R   Resources available to you to serve and you will be sustained by the power of spirit.

Y   Yield your fruits that have flourished during your labours and be at PEACE with yourself.

30th January, 1987

LOGOS

L   Love is the light of the world.

O   Obedience, to follow the pathway of light.

G   God, the Divine Spirit, the source of love.

O   Opportunity, to use the light to give help, comfort and strength.

S   Spirit, through acknowledgement of the spirit within, the love and light will shine out into the World, for the benefit of all mankind.

9th February, 1987

PRAYER

P   Pour out your worries, fears and troubles, let them be shared with God.

R   Relief, in knowing that the Love of God, can lift all burdens, causing light within to shine out into the world.

A   Accept, the truth of life, and move forward in your quest for knowledge of the spirit.

Y   Yearn, for the power of Love and Peace to conquer over the darkness in our World.

E   Enlightenment will follow and man will learn of the inner-self, enabling it to reveal the truth of Life.

Refuge is to be found in God, confide in the Love and know the PEACE profound.

16th February, 1987

PROGRESS

P   Pathway, the way of life that is chosen to fulfil the need from within.

R   Restrictions, the material pathway offers many restrictions, but all are lessons to strengthen the spirit.

O   Obstacles, will be removed as your spirit reaches forward to find the truth.

G   Goodness, will be the first fruit to be harvested as your pathway runs into the light of spiritual knowledge.

R   Rewards are to be gained through your new found spiritual strengths whereby you will be able to give to others unstintingly.

E   Eternity is the time in which you have to learn all the lessons of life, so you cannot fail.

S Search for the truth, a never ending task, seeking wisdom.

S Spirit is the light of the World, and the truth eternal.

22nd February, 1987

SPIRIT

S   Soul, your individuality and Divine spark within.

P   Progress, your soul must move forward to join as one with the Light of God.

I   Increase your awareness of the truth of life, through meditation.

R   Respond to the knowledge of your soul and follow the pathway of service.

I   Illumination is the outpouring of your soul, in love to all mankind.

T   Tranquillity, when your soul within is able to unite with the Divine Spirit, tranquillity of mind, body and spirit will prevail.

1st March, 1987

TRUTH

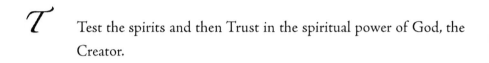

T   Test the spirits and then Trust in the spiritual power of God, the Creator.

R   Receive the knowledge of your spirit within, and understand yourself.

U   Unite your soul with the Universal God, and find inner peace.

T   Teach others of the natural laws which govern the Universe, allowing them to have access to the key, which will unlock the door, giving . . . .

H   Hope, so never despair, in the face of adversity, know the TRUTH, Life is eternal.

7th March, 1987

HARMONY

H   Higher consciousness, your true self, it should be allowed expression in this material world.

A   Allow your mind, body and soul to function as one, and all your actions should be in love.

R   Reserve your judgements of others and try to treat those you meet as your equal, whatever their caste or creed.

M   Material difficulties of life can be stressful to the soul but you, the individual, will progress spiritually through the hard lessons of life.

O   Obey your intuition and always remain positive in your thoughts, especially in the face of adversity.

N   Nature is the looking glass of the Divine Spirit, so stand back and observe the wonders of God.

Y   You are part of God, the Creator of Life, and when you understand this and live accordingly to the natural laws the whole world will benefit greatly.

15th March, 1987

HEALING

H   Help is at hand to lift the burdens of life from your shoulders, so look to God the Divine power.

E   Endurance of physical pain and sorrow will be eased, when you have found the key of eternal life, and your mind, body and soul unite as one, allowing your spirit to rise above adversity, bringing peace within.

A   Alone, you must understand that you are not alone in your suffering and your spiritual self will reveal to you the greatest gift of all, that of Love, which is God.

L   Learn from the knowledge of your spirit within and you will know that nothing dies, your physical body has only a limited life span, but your spirit is whole and its life is eternal.

I   Insight of eternal life will put the pressures of day to day living into perspective and you must understand that the physical body is just the vehicle in which we undertake the necessary journey in order to progress further in our understanding of the truth.

*N*ow is the time to impart the knowledge that you have attained and to prepare the way for others, so that they also may find contentment in their lives, and feel upliftment from the physical burdens of life.

*G*o forward on your pathway and lead by example in your way of life, just as those spiritual masters before us. By example you will endeavour to bring spirituality to the fore, in this material world and it will give comfort, strength and upliftment to everyone you meet, whatever their need.

20th March, 1987

MIND

M   Magnificent is the potential within each one of us. The spirit must be nurtured and acknowledged, so that it may flourish and be brought to the fore. Then you will realise that the power within, is the essence of life. Your light will shine into the World, if you just stop, look and listen to the still, small voice.

I   Intense is the power that you have become aware of. Therefore you must be instructed in its use. It should be treated with respect and never used for personal gain or self-esteem. Always remember the power is from God and is governed by the natural laws.

N   Negligence of the promptings of the spirit within is no excuse to push aside the truth. Truth has many facets but the gifts of the spirit are evident in our daily lives and must be given expression. Therefore, these gifts will not go unnoticed for God is working within each one of us. We are all part of the Great Spirit and light will always shine through the darkness of this material world.

D   Determination is required in our quest to lead a spiritual life in this material world. The pathway is a narrow and lonely one. Everything must balance, so discipline is to be exercised at all times. The growth of spiritual understanding may seem slow, but do not despair, for the spirit will reach its ultimate goal, that of instilling LOVE into the hearts of all mankind.

30th March, 1987

LOVE

L Life is eternal, and when this fact is accepted by man, then the material school room of learning will endeavour to teach of all things, both spiritual and material, and understanding of this truth will come about.

O Obstinate is the will of man, but the power of the spirit will overcome man's folly and the light will always shine out into the darkness, which is created by negative thoughts.

V Victorious is the Divine power of God the Creator of the Universe, over the creeds and dogmas of man, for the spirit within will always search for knowledge and truth.

E Entrust your soul to God, and develop and use your spiritual gifts to serve others. So live your earthly life according to the teachings of spirit and remember God is LOVE.

1st April, 1987

RESPONSIBILITY

R   Receptive. We should all be receptive to the promptings of the spirit within but many shun away from their inner feelings and push them aside. The first step is to acknowledge the spirit and begin a journey of discovery.

E   Embark on this journey with fortitude, for there will be many difficulties. Be guided by your own conscience and do what you know is right. Always act in Love.

S   Seek for truth. Your understanding of the truth will alter as your knowledge is widened. Through your increased knowledge you will find growing contentment and many answers to help you in the frustrations encountered in your material life.

P   Pursue your spiritual path with perseverance and all obstacles will be overcome. Do not judge your progress with that of others for it cannot be measured by comparison.

O   Observe the turmoil and strife in the World and do not be dismayed, know that the spirit is making progress within the hearts of mankind. The spirit must have freedom in this material world and when freedom is attained then peace will follow.

N   Needs. Your needs will be met but your desires are not the same as your needs. If you look back on your life you will know that having surmounted many problems your inner needs were fulfilled and materially too, a lesson was learnt.

S   Strength. You are stronger as a result of your experiences, whether they have been happy or sad. As you learn to share your burdens and joys you will know that your foundations are firm when built upon the eternal truth that life is everlasting.

I   Initially, you may be hesitant to reveal to others what you receive through meditation. Remember that by sharing you will grow in confidence and your knowledge and understanding of spiritual communication will develop.

B Be yourself, know yourself, for then your link with the Divine power will strengthen. You will find that no challenge will be too great when service to others is your goal, giving help wherever or whenever it is required. You cannot fail in this quest but you must always be in complete control of your actions.

I Instrument. You are an instrument for the work of God, the Divine Spirit. In understanding yourself and permitting your inner self to be expressed, go forward in love and you will accomplish your inner most desire, which is to free others from the bondage of ignorance.

L Look to God, the light. You cannot be of service to others if it is only for your own esteem. You must serve mankind as an ambassador for God and you are not entitled to be acknowledged for you are just an observer of the wonders that can be performed.

I Ignited is the flame of Love within you. Let it burn freely in order to inspire others to follow your way of life. This flame is kindled by the Divine power and as you give so shall you receive.

*T*ry your very best to live a full life and be proud of your achievements for this earthly life is strewn with many difficulties. Do not be boastful, remember your gifts are from God. Use them wisely.

*Y*ou are part of the Universe and have your place therein. Therefore man must respect the earth and not abuse its natural resources, you are its custodian. Be at PEACE with God, the Divine Power, the Creator of all Life.

6th April, 1987

KNOWLEDGE

K   Kindergarten. Our life on this earth is but a kindergarten, a schoolroom for learning, where our elected lessons may be experienced. Through these lessons, hard though they be, we progress slowly along this material pathway.

N   Necessity. Your earthly life is a necessity for spiritual progress, for you have much to learn and understand. As you live your life understanding will result from your experiences. You must experience life to be able to have understanding of it.

O   Onward. The direction in which to travel, towards the Light of the Divine Spirit. As you move forward in your understanding, the material and spiritual aspects of your life, will blossom and grow, just as the fruits of the earth respond to the laws of nature, so we must respond to the inner spirit.

W   Wisdom is the fruit of understanding, gained through your experiences, and is found deep within, therefore always available to you. Love is the key that unlocks the door to the wisdom of the Divine

Spirit. Many search for understanding, but if you do not search within, then wisdom cannot be found.

L Liberal. Be liberal in your thinking. Do not be held back by creeds, dogmas and fears. Your mind should always be open, ready to receive more and more as you become a channel for spiritual communication.

E Embark on the road to spiritual understanding. Accept that your existence is continuous, spirit cannot die. You are spirit here and now, clothed in a physical body. When you lose your physical body, your spirit is free to return to the realms of light. You have nothing to fear when you meet with the death of your earthly body.

D Dedicate your life to helping others along this pathway and by example lead them forward to know and experience the Divine spark within. They too will want to seek for truth and so the light of understanding will grow brighter and brighter, emanating peace and love into the whole World.

G Guidance is always close at hand. Seek and you will find. Never feel alone, answers will always be given. You are taught and guided in your dreams and meditation, so do not dismiss what has been given to you for everything you learn is important to your progress.

E Encouragement. You will always receive encouragement to move forward in your understanding, to use your gifts and talents wisely in order that many, many people will benefit from them. Be positive in your outlook and know the love of God is close at hand.

13th April, 1987

POWER

P   Prepare yourself for the truth, you cannot die, life is eternal, the spirit within is your true self and is your link with the spirit world. By acknowledging this fact you will wish to open your heart and mind towards the light, in order to become a channel for service.

O   Obey your intuition, which is always prompting you towards the light, when you face difficulties and will give you comfort, help and strength. Then having conquered your own shortcomings you will be equipped to pass on all you have learnt to those who are ready to listen.

W   Work endlessly with this light, use it to provide comfort, and healing to those in need. Rely on the Divine Power which is channelled through you, it will not let you down. When combined with your positive thoughts and actions, the impact of God's love towards mankind will not go unnoticed.

E   Experience is gained through living your material life, so learn by your mistakes. You must accept that you are responsible for all your thoughts and actions, whether good or bad and everything will have a reaction on how you feel. Therefore discipline yourself and be tolerant of others.

*R*esurrection of your soul from the physical body is what you term death but it is this process whereby the physical body returns to the earth and the soul to the world of spirit, its true home. Life is eternal and the world yearns for this truth, so spread the word, walk in the light of love—the power of God.

20th April, 1987

THOUGHTS

T   Try to quieten your mind to prepare the channel whereby you can achieve communication with your spirit within enabling you to pass on what you have learnt in the stillness of meditation to others.

H   Hinder. Do not allow negative ideas to hinder your meditation and wander away from the light. Be positive and your material life and spiritual life will benefit, for the pathways must run parallel in order for harmony to reign.

O   Opinion. Your opinion is important, it is your belief and you should be able to express it with zeal. But remember, keep your mind open for truth changes as your understanding of life increases.

U   Understand yourself, how you react and cope with life. You cannot understand others and give help to them, if you do not try to understand and deal with your own needs and weaknesses. Look within and find strength to face all adversity.

G   Give freely to others, be generous with your prayers. As you sow so shall you reap. The results will be good when you sow the seeds of Love, for the harvest will bring peace, comfort and healing to those who reach out for help.

H   Harmony within yourself is the key to success for you will be able to overcome all difficulties when your mind, body and spirit can act together bringing healing and strength to the fore. This inner peace is attained as a result of a positive approach.

T   Trust in yourself and in the power of the Divine Spirit, then there will be no barriers to overcome, and your channel will be fully open enabling spirit to work through you to shine light into this world, which seems obsessed with the darkness.

S   Silence. Retreat into the silence for it is here you will find the encouragement and strength to go forward in your quest. God will be found within, waiting patiently for us to acknowledge his great POWER, that of LOVE.

4th May, 1987

GOLD

G   Gifts. Acknowledge, understand and use your gifts for the benefit of yourself and others. Do not ignore or stifle them, allow them to develop and they will grow as your channel opens when more is added unto you. As you give of yourself, so shall you receive. Everything has its price, but do not count the cost of your labours. Reward is earned by love. Love, is the link between the two worlds and it will never let you down, you cannot fail, for the power of God is Love.

O   Observe as you live your life and learn from each experience. Through observation comes increased awareness and understanding so be alert to everything around you both materially and spiritually. Changes are constant in life and take time in your meditation to understand the lessons that you have to learn. Take each step slowly, have patience, do not rush your development for spiritual awakening is an eternal process. The purpose of this earthly life is to awaken the spirit within.

L   Look forward do not hold on to the past. You must move towards the Light, for this is progress. The past cannot be changed, whatever experiences you have encountered, you have moved forward along your chosen path. You are in control, and by positive thinking, take charge of your life. You are responsible for your own deeds, actions and thoughts. So be at peace within yourself and your future will be one of contentment. One step further is being able to give this peace to others and this is true fulfilment. Therefore, strive for this goal.

D Discipline is required to keep a balance in your life. With discipline you can master all the pressures of life, therefore nothing can stand in your way, of YOU reaching the ultimate goal of acting as a channel to prove God's love of mankind. Remember you have your part to play in this tapestry of life and each act which gives expression of the Light, by your deeds or thoughts, is one step forward in the quest for truth to manifest itself. Truth is eternal life, and eternal life is truth. This is the hardest lesson of life for mankind to understand.

9th May, 1987

NATURE

N Nothing comes from nothing. Everything comes from the life force, which is God. God is everything and in order to understand this great truth, we must live in harmony. When harmony prevails then full expression of love will follow. As you gain knowledge and understanding of yourself, the wisdom of life will be unfolded from within and peace is the key to unlock the door to harmony and love.

A Abandon all creed and dogma from your mind. Keep your mind open to receive the wisdom hidden deep within and then question all that is imparted to you, in order to grow in understanding. Accept what you feel is truth and do not worry over things, as yet beyond your comprehension. By looking within for the answers you are slowly progressing along the pathway of true enlightenment. Ask and you shall receive, seek and you will find. Strive for happiness and find peace within yourself.

T Termination. There is no termination of life, no end. Life is continuous, you cannot die, you will live forever, but your physical body will not be required when you leave this physical world and enter the world of spirit. This transition is a natural one. You will be delighted with your experiences in this new dimension of life and death should not be feared. Until mankind takes the trouble to realise that life does not end when the physical body ceases to function, then man will continue to fight man over trivialities of differing beliefs in the name of God and religion.

U Unity of mankind is the aim of the spirit world. We live on the earth to progress and learn the lessons necessary for our awareness of God to grow within and be acknowledged. We must learn to live together in harmony and love. First of all we must try to understand ourselves and then we can begin to understand others. Through nations gaining understanding of the spirit within then discord and strife will disappear and unity of thought between mankind will become a reality and love will conquer all. The time this might take is not important for all changes should be made slowly. There is no time limit we have Eternity.

R Reflection. We are all a reflection of our concept of God. We can hide behind our actions towards our fellow man, but not behind our thoughts. We are as we think, this is our true self, so be positive in your thinking and extend love towards those you meet. Do not be hurt by the actions of others, look further than appearances, and know your true friends. The colour of skin and other physical attributes should not divide mankind, for we are all equal, in that we are part of God. We all should have knowledge of that inner Divine spark. The light within is constantly shining and by this light we are known.

E Eternity, forever. Therefore, time cannot limit your progress for time is limitless. You have enough time—eternity—in which to accomplish your ambitions. You should not measure your spiritual progress in earthly time, have patience. As this World responds to the Love of God and obeys the natural laws, it is then that the true spirituality of mankind will manifest on the Earth, allowing harmony and peace expression, when love will accomplish true perfection of paradise on Earth.

17th May, 1987

PROTECTION

P   Power. Use the power of the spirit, found within, for the benefit of yourself and others. Through meditation and prayer you can encompass the two Worlds, for when you open the channel, your spirit is allowed expression. It is only then that you will begin to understand the deeper meaning of life and with uncertainty as you step forward into the unknown you will be guided. By understanding yourself you will be able to offer comfort and help to others. Love is the key to full understanding of life and will banish all our fears.

R   Restore a balance in your life so that you may feel the harmony within. Learn to quieten your mind and find time to listen to the still small voice. As you are able to adjust your thinking to accommodate your new ideas, you will see your material difficulties in a different light and positive thought combined with inner peace will create a 'whole' person. When your mind, body and spirit harmonize then you may live a full life. Remember you have free will, and must live your physical life as you desire, you are responsible for all your actions.

O   Obligation. Your first obligation is to yourself. You cannot run away from the fact that you have to live with yourself. All your thoughts and actions you are responsible for—no one else can undertake your responsibilities for you. Find yourself, know yourself and then you will be able to give help to all those who expect you to oblige their needs. Help can be imparted to others in many different ways and their burdens must not become yours. Therefore you must learn to detach yourself, and stand back slightly, in order to allow spirit to work through you as a channel to fulfil their needs.

T Treasure the moments of quietness and use the time to strengthen your spirit. In this our world today, the pace of life is hectic and only a few moments in prayer, each day, will give you the uplift you need to carry out your daily commitments. Meditation and prayer opens the door to the spirit world, where you can leave your troubles, where you can rest a while to recuperate from the effects of stress of all the physical demands made upon you. Be disciplined in your life and make time each day for prayer and meditation.

E Enable your spirit within to grow and to expand. Enter into the silence and there find peace. Peace can only be acquired through your own efforts and peace within will allow the spirit freedom. Your spirit cannot be confined in your physical form forever, as it is constantly searching for expression. Once we have acknowledged the existence of our spirit, it is then that the channel is opened and we can use this power to sustain us and also pass it on to help others. We are all given gifts and must understand and use them in order to bring healing, comfort and love into this material world, for the benefit of all mankind.

C Custodians. We are custodians of this planet Earth and we should not abuse its natural resources. We must try to live in harmony with nature and especially with the animals that also inhabit this earth plane. We seem to think that we have sole rights to everything on this planet and man fights man in order to own more land. True wealth cannot be counted by worldly possessions and this is a hard lesson to learn. True wealth is found in the richness of your spirit for it is your spirit that lives on. Your spirit is you, how you think, how you feel, and you build on this as you progress. If you understand things of the spirit whilst living on this earth, then the light within is allowed expression and is ready to move forward with strength into its natural home, the World of Spirit.

T Temptation. This physical world is full of temptation to divert you away from the spiritual pathway of life. Our lives are arduous, it is a constant battle. We must survive, we must win pressure is on for everyone to be a winner in the material stakes. We are thus tempted by all the trappings of materialism and in trying to become a winner, there is no time left to make inroads into the spiritual values. We should know instinctively of the spiritual essence of life, as we all have spiritual experiences during the sleep state, but when the time is right, the spiritual awakening within man will come about and the material temptations will be overcome. Then with the harmony of the physical and spiritual worlds acting in unison, the truth of the spirit will be made known to man.

I Illustrate to the World the true harmony of the both Worlds functioning as one. When you have found the peace and harmony within and are able to share your knowledge with others, you will grow in understanding. Then by your actions as well as your thoughts you will be able to show something of your true self to others, and your inner light will ignite the Divine spark within them. Many Masters who have had a true balance in their understanding of eternal life have inspired man to look within for knowledge and wisdom and now it is our task to lead by example, giving love to all those we meet and looking within for deeper knowledge and understanding.

O Obsession. In gaining understanding of yourself you should not become obsessed by truth. Always keep an open mind for truth changes with increased understanding. Remember too, that everyone has a right to their expression of the truth and many roads lead to the understanding of the great truth that Life is eternal. Therefore be patient in your quest for truth and live your life by displaying the knowledge you have gained. Keep your standards high, aim for the harmony of peace and love within and use your spiritual gifts for the benefit of others and your positive approach to life will outweigh all material strife. Learn from the hard lessons of this physical life, that love can never die and love is your bond with those whose home is the spirit world.

No one is lost in the sea of life. Everyone must move forward. We are all reluctant to leave our physical bodies, for our body has become familiar to us and we do not understand the freedom we will gain when it returns to the earth and our spirit returns to the realms of light. Your spirit will prepare you for this transition and all fears will subside when the release is made. We grieve the loss of a loved one to the spirit world but remember it is our love that enables them to communicate with us, so do not stifle that love allow your spirit communion with theirs and acknowledge their presence. Love is God and God is love, so know deep within that everyone has the opportunity to enjoy a full life in the spiritual dimension of light and love.

25th May, 1987

LIFE FORCE

L Light is the pure vibration of Love. Look towards the light for the truth, seek and you will find. If you walk your pathway in the light of spiritual understanding and acknowledge the power within, then you will be able to open the channel to enable your 'light', your spirit within to shine into the darkness of this material world. As your inner self grows then love will blossom forth and through love you will be able to help many people who are ready to accept the love you impart. Love is God, so any act or thought performed in love will enlighten those who seek a deeper understanding of life.

I Illusion. Life on the earth plane is a series of hard lessons. If you think that life begins at physical birth and ends in physical death, as is the view of the majority, you are living in a world of illusion. The reality of life is that it is eternal, and spiritually you will never die. The physical world is an illusion for nothing is as it appears. To find reality look within and seek the truth of life. Your spirit is seeking knowledge and understanding of spiritual truths that will help lift the burdens you bear. You can only move forward along the pathway of life and as you learn your lessons so you progress and your true inner self is strengthened.

F Freedom. You must allow your spirit freedom. It must not be confined, it cannot be confined for it is the 'real' you. If your spirit cannot find expression then you will find that your life is unbalanced, you may become ill, and nothing can alleviate your pain and suffering. Therefore find peace within and by understanding yourself your spirit will respond by imparting to you a feeling of harmony. As your spirit grows the light glows ever brighter. Work with the light of spirit and use your spiritual gifts wisely. Always act in love offering help and comfort to those in need. With a free spirit, harmony and peace can be yours forever and your whole being will emanate love to all.

E Escape. You cannot escape from the truth that life is eternal, and live in ignorance and fear. You will have to learn the lessons you have elected whilst on this Earth, which is a school room well equipped for teaching us. The lessons will not be easy, but help is always close at hand. Take each experience and learn from it and as you gain knowledge and understanding, you will slowly move forward along life's pathway. Remember, you are master of your own destiny and fully responsible for every thought and action you perform. No one can carry the burdens of life for you, but your true self—your inner spirit—will provide you with the power you require to overcome all the obstacles on your path. Meet every challenge with fortitude and know that you will find your reward in gaining a deeper understanding of your spirit within and of the Divine plan that life is eternal.

F Fellowship. Find fellowship with others, for truth must be shared. When you have sought understanding and guidance from within, then the time will come, as you move forward, when your knowledge must be imparted to others, who also wish to seek for truth. As you share so shall you learn for we all have different spiritual gifts. Accept help from others and receive graciously what has been imparted to you. Know that sharing is natural to the spirit, but selfishness hinders the work of the Divine Spirit. Mankind should be a fellowship sharing the resources of this Earth as well as those spiritual gifts but man will not share true fellowship until he learns tolerance. Selfishness must give way to selflessness, when life on Earth would become a paradise of peace and love.

O Obstruct. You cannot obstruct the Divine plan for the natural laws will always govern the universe. By the same token you cannot obstruct your own progress along the pathway of life and whatever obstacles you encounter you will not move backwards, the only direction in which to move is forwards into a greater understanding. Many have tried to stand in the way of spiritual progress, but failed in their quest to extinguish the light. The light within man will continue to shine and nothing will ever totally obscure that light. When the spirit within is burning brightly, then love, harmony and peace will always overcome the darkness of our World today. As soon as we acknowledge the Divine Spirit then the Divine Plan takes a step forward in its quest for true enlightenment of spirit to manifest itself within our physical world.

R Reflect your inner spiritual light into our material world. Use your spiritual gifts to ignite the Divine spark within others enabling them to go forward seeking truth. The reflection of your light is seen by others as all your actions are coloured by your thoughts. Draw on your light and use the power to give healing, comfort and peace to others and know that everyone can benefit from your efforts. Keep your own counsel be positive in your thinking. Do not allow your inner light to grow dim, through physical demands, find time to rekindle the flame, through meditation and prayer. Use the light and let it glow brighter and brighter as you impart God's love to mankind.

C Contained within you is the ability to recognise God. You are part of God, and as soon as you look within and find understanding of yourself, you will also obtain an understanding of God. A deity, named God cannot change the World for us, and suddenly create harmony amongst mankind. We are responsible for ourselves and until harmony is acquired within by each individual, then peace and love cannot be paramount in the World. Therefore the onus is on mankind and man must not blame God for the dreadful plight that man finds himself in. The answer to the strife, famine and disease is quite simple. Each individual must acquire harmony, healing and peace within himself and only then will the whole world benefit from Love.

E Extract from life all that you desire, for life is for living, but do not hurt others by your actions as you take what you consider to be yours. In order to partake in life's tapestry you must live your own life, giving freely of yourself, breaking down all the barriers built through fear and ignorance. Learning by experience is the only way to refine your soul and as you give so you shall receive. Therefore, know that you can stand up to all the challenges that confront you when you understand and utilise the power of the Divine Spirit. Walk in the light of Divine Love and many will follow in your footprints, in order to seek for truth. By knowing yourself you create inner happiness and in knowing yourself you know God, who is the creator of life eternal.

1st June, 1987

RHYTHM

R   Regulate. The natural laws regulate the power of the Universe, which vibrates on many different levels. These vibrations penetrate all things and gives life to everything. The Universe has many different spheres and each sphere vibrates at a higher or lower speed. The vibration of the physical sphere, the Earth plane, is slow, due to the denseness of matter and the vibration of the spiritual sphere is much faster. We have the natural ability to higher our consciousness in order to experience the many different levels of the power of the spirit and in doing so may have communion with our friends, relatives and loved ones, who have left this physical life and now exist in the vibration of light and love.

H   Harmony. When you find harmony within yourself then you will be able to emanate the vibration of love from your heart. The vibration of love is the key to the truth of eternal life and as you harmonize with the natural laws in your way of living, as well as in your thinking, then you will begin to grow in knowledge and understanding of the Divine Plan. Find time in your day to unite your thoughts with the Universal Spirit, through prayer and meditation. As a result of your daily prayers so the burdens of your material life will be eased by the increased strength, gained through your mind, body and spirit, being given the time to unite and function as a whole. Know that the veil of death is but the beginning of life anew in a World of Light and love where your soul will have full life.

*Y*ou are responsible for your own life and it is important that you take charge. When taking charge, do not become selfish and self-centred, be positive and live your life to the full, always being aware of those around you. One of the first lessons to be learnt is to accept the natural law of cause and effect. This is a hard lesson, but answers many questions as regards this chaotic world of ours. This earth is suffering greatly as man thinks that all its natural resources are his for the taking, but this is not so. As man takes from the earth, he is altering the natural balance and this is the cause of the many disasters. Balance your life and peace and harmony will override the disease and strife, and when mankind can accept a life where balance must prevail, then the earth will recover its beauty and function naturally. When mankind is enlightened to this fact then disease and famine will be alleviated and peace will overcome strife.

*T*empo. The tempo of your life should be steady, as steady as the beat of your heart. Find time to be calm, and let the World rush by, devote a few moments each day to your spiritual needs. You will find that as soon as you can regulate the tempo your physical body will be able to function naturally, that is in harmony with your mind and spirit. When you allow this to happen then sickness of the physical body will lessen and you will become 'whole'. It is not an easy task to accomplish, for the mind, body and spirit vibrate at different speeds. Remember that through meditation and prayer, you allow the spirit within to flow freely. From the freedom of spirit you will find harmony and peace within your heart, so build on this foundation and impart the knowledge and understanding of truth to all mankind.

H Healing of the physical body from disease must come from within, where the cause is always found. When the spirit within is touched by power of the Divine Spirit then healing takes place. Recovery may not be instant, but slowly the spirit within responds. Physically the body may not improve, but this does not signify failure, for the mind and spirit of the sick person will benefit and be strengthened by the great power of love and be freed from the physical body to live a full life within the World of Spirit. We may all become healing channels for spirit by using our thoughts. The recipient of our healing prayers does not have to know or believe in the power of thought to benefit. All who require healing will receive according to their needs and no one is forgotten. Disease is caused through disharmony within and mankind causes much suffering to one another through fighting and wars. Remember that you may be able to hurt the physical body but man's spirit is eternal and can never be destroyed.

M Music is soothing and helps to quieten the mind. Your mind is powerful in itself but must be repressed a little, with the aid of gentle music, to allow the spirit within expression. Music that is soft and pleasant allows you to spend a few moments within yourself, where you can experience the harmony and peace and when you are relaxed then you free your spirit in order to search for truth. The vibration of soft music will dissolve your material worries, for a little while, and then your mind and spirit will be free to experience many things, bringing to you a much deeper understanding of life and giving to you peace. Peace within is a truly wonderful gift and many souls on the Earth never experience it. If you can attain peace within for just one fleeting moment, then you will be able to say, from your heart, that you have found God and God has found you.

7th June, 1987

PATHWAY

P   Progress. As you live your life so you progress in one direction—
forwards, in the struggle to understand yourself. By understanding
yourself so spiritual progress begins. Look within and then project
your thoughts outwards. What you will find within is the key to
eternal life, you will come face to face with your soul, your true self,
which is eternal. By finding your inner self, your soul, you have begun
your quest for knowledge. Then when you combine knowledge with
understanding, wisdom is infused from your soul, and you will feel
compelled to pass it on to others. Remember, by thought alone you
can unite with others, so when you acknowledge the power within,
and begin to use the great potential of your soul, the love will be
given freely to those in need, and they will benefit greatly. As your
soul strives for expression always use your gifts with reverence. Each
experience encountered in your material life will refine your soul.
Therefore do not despair when facing adversity, learn from your
difficulties and know that you are receiving help and guidance in
your time of need. Ask and you shall receive, and as you seek so shall
you find. You learn from experience and you know from experience
that the Divine Spirit, Love, is to be found within you.

A   Awareness. By meditation and entering into that inner silence you
will be able to search within your soul to find the answers you are
seeking. As you open your mind to accept the deeper meaning of life,
so your awareness and understanding of the truth begins. Practise

meditation daily and during this time discard all your material worries. Find peace in your meditation and allow your spirit freedom to guide you in your quest for knowledge and truth. Remember, you are always in control during your meditation, and you will be able to see deeper into the light of knowledge as your understanding of truth expands and you experience peace to be found within. This inner peace will allow your material life to become less restrictive and it will unlock your mind from the creeds and dogmas imposed upon you by the society in which you live. Meditation will prepare you to accept the truth that life is eternal, and during meditation you must strive to move forward into the light of greater understanding, thus allowing peace to blossom from within your soul.

*T*ruth. The truth of life has many different facets. Be disciplined in your thinking as you meditate and open your mind to receive knowledge and understanding of eternal life. Truth is hindered by your understanding. Truth cannot change for it is fundamental to life, but your understanding of truth does change as your mind accepts the knowledge freely imparted by your true inner self, your soul. Do not judge others on their beliefs for there are many roads that lead you to the truth that your spirit will free itself from the physical body when you die, and will continue its journey in the spiritual world of light, the light of Love and understanding. This eternal truth should inspire men to live as brothers on this earth and to live in peace and harmony with one another, and this is what man should be striving for in his material life, but first he must find peace within himself, in his spiritual quest, and then project it outwards into his material life, before man will be able to live together as a Brotherhood.

H Humility. Be humble in your attitude. You are responsible for your own thoughts and actions, so keep at peace with yourself. Through meditation you have developed your spiritual gifts, which are to be used for the benefit of others. You cannot choose your gifts and the gifts bestowed upon you have been earned, so accept these gifts in humility. By opening your heart and mind you become a channel for spirit to work through you. Having allowed yourself to be used as a channel many, many people will ask for your help. Do you fail them, be disciplined in your way of life, in order that you may commit yourself wholeheartedly to the work of God, allowing love to flow through you freely. The gifts of the spirit, are not always understood, by those seeking help. Show patience and love for help will be given to all who ask, and you are the channel, through which God's love can be bestowed on them. Do not question what help is given, for it is not your place, spirit knows the need of the seeker and you must trust in God's love.

W Weakness. Do not be afraid of your weaknesses. Out of weakness comes strength to overcome all obstacles. If we did not acknowledge our weaknesses then we would not look within for strength. As you move forwards in your material life you need physical strength and in your spiritual life, you need spiritual strength. Be positive in your thinking, do not be afraid of yourself. You cannot fail, for the road is eternal. When the physical body becomes weak, the spirit within is strengthened. Your spirit is eternal, and it is strengthened by the Divine power of Love. If you build your material life on the sure foundation of Love, then you will feel at one with God, as your spirit prepares to leave your physical body. Death is not to be feared, for it is but the beginning of life anew. A life whereby nothing is hidden, for now everything has a wider perspective, and is seen as a whole. Weakness is overcome and strength is gained from Love.

A Attempt to live at one with God. Strive to know yourself, through meditation. Knowing yourself is knowing God and finding harmony and peace within is the first step towards living in harmony with the natural laws. As you move forward in your quest for deeper understanding put your knowledge into action by bringing harmony to mankind. If you can live at peace with yourself then encourage mankind to live at peace with each other. Try to influence others by example. Peace is the answer that many people strive to find for it is the key to allow your spirit within expression. The spirit within, having found peace, will enkindle the flame of Love. As this flame of love burns within so you must use it to offer light to those who walk in the darkness. Light is love and love is God. If you can shine your light into the World, by your thoughts as well as your actions, then love is expressed towards mankind and you and God are one.

Y Yes, love is eternal, for it cannot be destroyed. It is your link with the spiritual force of light and power, so give of your love to others and as you give so shall you receive. Love is given to us all. Love is kindness, love is thoughtfulness, love is caring, so demonstrate love to those you meet in your daily life. Love blossoms from man's heart, from deep within. The seed of love grows towards the light of spiritual understanding, gained through the experience of life. Always keep your faith in the power of love and do not under estimate it for love is God and God is love and love is constantly at work within the Universe. Love will never be extinguished or smothered by the darkness of ignorance and fear, for the spirit within is always striving towards the light of understanding. It is your responsibility, to lead by example and to demonstrate the gifts of the spirit to give help, comfort and strength to those in need and for the many who are searching to find peace and truth.

22nd June, 1987

AWARENESS

A Attune yourself to the vibration of love and know that love is your link with the World of Spirit and with mankind. We are all equal in our quest to understand ourselves and the Universe in which we live. Mankind is searching and striving for knowledge but only those who are prepared to look within themselves find the key that will unlock the door the truth that life is eternal. This key is love, the essence of God, and with this key open your heart and mind to enable your spirit to grow in the light of love. As your spirit responds to the love of God, so it will flourish and blossom. It is then that your channel will open, allowing you to give to others what you have received from entering the silence within. By example and experience you will be able to show many the pathway that leads you to find truth, through your own efforts, without being bound by dogma and creeds. Look at yourself and be true to yourself, giving love to all.

W When you begin to search for truth, you will find the road narrow and long. Prepare yourself for this great journey, by entering the silent world within, where you may meditate. There you will experience many, many things, as your mind unites with your spirit and the channel for communication is opened to the world of light and love. You must allow your mind to remain open to the truth, so never let it shut out the light of truth and knowledge, for if your mind is undisciplined it will begin to fight against the light for fear of the truth. Your mind in order to function naturally should have a full understanding of the spirit within and then your physical body too would benefit greatly from your mind and spirit being in harmony and disease and illness would be overcome. Everyone is searching for truth and it is your mind which is the filter. Your mind is part of you and you have complete control of it, you are responsible for all your actions and thoughts and your spirit cannot over rule your mind.

A Attentive. Be attentive to your own progress and look upon it as a garden, allowing your spirit to reach full blossom. Your spirit is like a seed which has been planted and it needs its share of sunshine and showers in order to grow in strength. The showers of life are the sadness and crying and the sunshine is the happiness and laughter. As you experience these emotions so the spirit within begins to respond and strives towards the light, in order to reach its full potential of becoming a beautiful flower. The light is the spiritual light of love and as you experience the Divine power of love within yourself, so your spirit will blossom and open in order to receive the love of the spirit world. Then when your spirit opens fully you will be able to impart that love to others who are in need of upliftment. You will feel the power of love when you unite with your inner self and you will know that through your thoughts as well as your actions you can offer help to the many who are in need. Your garden is symbolic of your spirit, do not neglect it, for through neglect a garden becomes a wilderness of weeds and overgrowth, and the flowers are hidden. Tend to your spirit and your garden will be a beautiful place where you will find pleasure and peace.

R Respond to the promptings of your spirit. You have many books to read and understand about the truth of life, but do not accept without question what you read or are told by others. Your spirit is your true self and it is just waiting for you to accept the truth that it can impart to you. In knowing yourself and accepting truth you will be able to understand the simplicity of life. Your spirit knows and understands what it has to endure and experience during your life on this earth. In fact you have to accomplish many things during the allotted time, so listen carefully with your inner ear, and use the strength of your spirit to enable you to face all the challenges that life has to offer you. With love and fortitude there is nothing that you cannot bear. You cannot fail in life for love is the key of success. Remember, to live your life in harmony with your inner self and then you will find that with love in your heart you can live at peace with yourself and a happy, contented and peaceful life is yours, for peace is a gift from God.

E Endeavour to follow your inner light. This is not an easy task for we live in a material world. As we battle with our material difficulties we do, on occasions, allow the light within to grow dim, by pushing away the help that is offered. We forget all too quickly that the spirit within can sustain us when we are striving to overcome our material problems and therefore neglect the strength that is within. It is a very important lesson to learn that it is the spirit within that gives us the strength to move forward along the pathway of life, for the spirit within is the true self and spirit is a reality, for all that is material is but an illusion. So by following the light within you will see your life in its true perspective and soon will understand that material values are low and strive for spiritual values and know that the price is high. You earn your spiritual gifts so combine your material and spiritual pathways and offer those who seek, the harmony peace and strength found from the light within.

 Negative. Do not become negative in your outlook, for the negative forces of doubt and despondency are to be overcome. Positive thoughts can overcome all that is negative. Mankind seems satisfied to accept all that is negative, without question, but pushes aside the positive power of love. Love is eternal and it is love that will unite the world. First of all, man must find the love within himself and having found it must learn to project if out to encourage others to look and search for the truth of life. Everyone is searching for truth and help and guidance is needed for there are many who walk into darkness instead of the light and they need assistance. The darkness is but the other side of the same coin, the coin of love. Love is light and ignorance and hatred is darkness. Man must strive towards the light and through the experience of love comes understanding of the truth. Truth is within, love is within and doubt and ignorance and hatred, the darkness, cannot overcome the light of truth and love. Light dispels all darkness as you walk along the spiritual pathway of love.

 Essence. The essence of life is love. God is love, the Divine source of light. Without love we have nothing and with love we have everything. Love is within you and around you, for love is the link between the spiritual and material worlds. You must not use the link with spirit for your own material gain or boast of your spiritual gifts. Love must be used with humility for you are but the channel through which love may have expression in order to give help to those who are in need. You will be tested, and your inner spirit will know your motives, so always act in truth and love. Ensure that you serve others in love and your channel will always remain open, becoming wider as you grow in spiritual understanding, thus allowing your gifts to develop. Strive for this development but have patience. Understand yourself and know that you are spirit now and spirit is love. Love is God and you are part of God. It is your responsibility to give love to others freely, for it is freely given to you and must be utilised in this material world.

S Search diligently throughout your life, for truth has no end. Truth is eternal and although truth cannot change your understanding of truth will. Take each step on the pathway of development slowly, for you cannot rush your lessons. As you begin to search, you will find many questions you would like answered. Man has the natural ability to search and he will not rest until the answer is found. When one answer is found it will create another question and so a circle is formed, symbolising that truth has no beginning or end. In your search you will grow in understanding for you cannot move backwards in your quest for knowledge. Begin with yourself, for by knowing yourself, you will be able to give help to others. It is not a pleasant task, being honest with yourself, but it is where you must begin, in order to be of assistance to others. Know yourself, and you know God, so search deep within and you will find much to please, a place where you may listen to the still small voice and enjoy the harmony and peace found therein.

S Service. Having gained an understanding of your spiritual gifts it is your responsibility to use them in service to others. You must make that commitment and once you have made that decision then do not hesitate to move forward along your chosen path. Be disciplined with yourself in order to meet the many demands which will be made upon you. The task of serving others is a difficult one and you cannot turn anyone away, for you have committed yourself to give freely to others. However, you must find time to devote to yourself and your material life, for harmony within and around you is essential. Be in control of your life, and do not become too involved in the problems of others. You are the channel through which help is given to others, but it is not your place to take on the responsibilities of others, for they must live their own lives. Each person is only responsible for himself and personal responsibility is a hard task to accept. You can offer help as you meet others but do not forget to receive help, for we are all in need. As you give so shall you receive and by service to others you can lead by example.

29th June, 1987

MEDIUM

M   Maturity is the natural progress of growth, for everything moves forward towards the light for light is essential to growth. Therefore it is necessary for man to seek and follow in the light of truth and love. Mankind has to mature in three dimensions. His physical body will mature at a very fast rate, when it is nourished. His mentality will grow at a slightly slower pace and his mental body has to be stimulated in order to mature. His spiritual body will be the last to reach full maturity for it has to blend with the powerful physical and mental forces and needs the strength and discipline of both on which to depend. The spiritual body, the essential and eternal you, is striving for recognition. The physical body upon reaching maturity is the first to fall into decline and during its decline, so the mental and spiritual bodies are allowed to blossom. The spiritual body strengthens the mental body and so the unity of mind, body and spirit is what we seek, whilst the physical body is strong. However, when we do not feed the spiritual body with light, then it has to wait for the physical body to fail before it can begin to find the light and know the truth that life is eternal.

E   Engage in your search for truth wholeheartedly. Have patience in your quest for you are not limited by time. Understanding of truth is a gift in itself for truth is found in simplicity. Many roads will lead you to truth and you have the choice. Masters throughout the ages have attempted to show mankind how to find peace and contentment but man is slow to learn. Your search must begin within yourself, for you and God are one. When you understand yourself then you begin to understand the truth. Love is the key which unlocks the door to life, an internal life, for Love is God. As you find love within and live your life by giving expression to it, then you become an instrument for God. Remember, love is truth, so always use the great power of love with sincerity and in humility. Do not abuse or neglect your understanding of the truth but know that your search within gave you the key and you have many doors to open with that key for each door is symbolic of progress, progress towards the light of God.

D Duty. You have a duty to yourself, so find time to relax and enter the silence within. Do not be afraid to search within for it is here you will find your inner self, the Divine spark, the light of love, which is God. Each man is responsible for himself and within his physical body will find the Divine spirit. When you acknowledge this then you begin on the pathway of truth. You cannot run away from truth, yet many spend their physical lives fighting against the truth within. They stifle the promptings of the spirit, which causes unnecessary pain and suffering, instead of allowing the spirit freedom, the freedom to serve. Freedom of spirit will give health and strength to your body and you will be free to learn and acknowledge the many gifts of the spirit. Do not be afraid to seek for knowledge for it is stored within. Ask and you will receive, seek and you will find. When you have found inner peace, then your duty is no longer to yourself, but to others. In order to fulfil your duty you have to instil discipline into your life so that you can maintain your commitments when offering your spiritual gifts, for the benefit of all who are in need, demonstrating God's love to all mankind.

I Impart your knowledge and understanding and use your spiritual gifts to benefit others. Do not enforce your views but be willing to be of service to those who seek. You have a wealth of knowledge and experience which is individual to you and by giving of yourself to others and allowing yourself to be used as a channel for God's love to work through you many, many people will be drawn to the light of truth and understanding. As you give so you will receive and by using your gifts so you will progress slowly along your chosen pathway with fortitude and courage. You will be tested and your pathway will not be easy. Do not stumble or fall for you know the way and will be guided by your inner spirit and its strength will always sustain you throughout this arduous physical life. By your light you are known so allow your spirit to shine into the world, by giving of yourself to others, thus dispelling the darkness of ignorance and fear. Illumine your life by allowing your spiritual gifts to blossom and grow and you will ignite the souls of men to follow in the light of love.

U Unique. You are unique for you are an individual. Everyone is responsible for their own thoughts and actions and the spirit within, the inner self, your soul is unique, for it is but a part of God. Therefore, the spiritual gifts, which we all possess are unique within each individual but originate from the same source that of God. We have to discover this truth for ourselves and it becomes our personal responsibility to develop and use our gifts, to the best of our ability. Once we have acknowledged and accepted our pathway, then we may endeavour to use our knowledge and understanding to encourage others to look within themselves. Although we are all individual we are all part of a whole and we must strive to become part of the whole, whereby we will lose our individuality, for no man is an island and we are all dependant on one another. When mankind realises that he is not self sufficient but is dependant on the Divine power of God and that power is within himself, only then will harmony be found between all men.

M Man symbolises God. It is our personal responsibility to allow the spirit within to work through us offering service to others by using the gifts that we have developed. It is important to remember that we are all equal spiritually, there is no division for love is found within us all. We are only divided by creeds and dogma and through our lack of understanding of the different pathways that lead to the truth, the simplicity that life, in the spiritual sense is eternal. The spirit within, the love, coupled with our individuality combines and becomes the soul. The greater our awareness and understanding of the Divine Spirit the more knowledge there is to be gained along life's pathway of eternity. Never become complacent in your thinking for when mankind can acknowledge his soul and begins to live in harmony with himself and others and obeys the natural laws, then and only then will paradise be found on Earth, when PEACE and LOVE abound.

2nd August, 1987

COURAGE

C Challenge. Your life is a challenge, so draw on your inner strength in order to meet the demands made upon you. Never feel alone, for your inner self is your life line to the great power of God. Your spirit within is prepared for all that you have to face during your physical life span on this Earth. For it is during these years that you have many hard lessons to learn. Do not despair for deep within you have the fortitude and strength to win through and move closer towards the light. The first lesson to be learnt is that of knowing yourself. Look within for your inner self is the eternal you and once you have taken time to meet and understand yourself, you then have the essential tools with which to build on the firm foundation of love and then your channel will be open to demonstrate the gifts of the spirit.

O Obedience. Be obedient to the light, all your actions should be well meaning and for the benefit of others, and not for your own personal gain and advantage. You must serve others as you would wish others to serve you, for only then will the love be permitted to shine into this world of darkness and fear. You must live your life in obedience to all that is good and never stray from the pathway of light. If you can understand and accept this, you will realise that by living your life in accordance with the promptings of your soul, you will be able to deal with your life in a positive and constructive way, for your spirit is your guide, along life's uneven path and you must understand and trust your spirit within and live in obedience to it. It is YOU and YOU are it, so know the truth, that your life is eternal.

U Universal is God's love, it has no confines, for no dogma or creed can lay claim to it. It cannot be held by anyone or anything for love is within all. You have to find yourself and look within to find the spark of light. This spark is the essence of your spiritual life and whatever your caste, every man is equal for he has a spirit within seeking expression. The differences between man exist because the understanding of the spirit is at many different levels. Truth has to be found and to search for truth will bring about knowledge and then understanding. As each individual grows towards the light of truth, then love is expressed and its power is limitless, and so it will spread throughout the universe and is God's gift to all mankind. It is there for the taking, but must never be abused. Love is eternal and will never be destroyed by the darkness of ignorance and fear within our material world.

R Respond to this love, for it is your duty. Do not hesitate to follow your inner most thoughts for you are always close to the Divine Spirit, when you sit and pray for others and enter the silence within. During your meditation know the love is the tie that binds you to the world of spirit and light and live your life by knowing and understanding the fundamental truth that you cannot die, for you will always be able to live a full life as long as you have love. Love, not for self but for others and by expressing love, so your thoughts go out into the ether and combine with the spiritual force of love. As you give of yourself so you will receive, for as your capacity for love expands and your light within grows brighter, so it will illumine your pathway and will give you the strength to cope with life. Never despair for love conquers all, act in love and the response is felt within your heart.

 Ascend the many levels of consciousness in your quest for truth, for there is much to learn. Take great care and prepare yourself for meditation. Meditation is a skill to be mastered and the rewards are great. Enter your meditation as a child, without fear and with trust. In the silence of meditation meet with your teacher, who is known to you. Your teacher is waiting to instruct you and you must be eager and willing to learn. Never doubt the simplicity of the lesson for it is only made difficult by the fact that our minds are narrowed by the pressures of the material world. As we learn and understand the spiritual lessons, during meditation, the test of our progress is measured during our physical life span. So meet your joys and sorrows with fortitude and grace, for it is only through experience that you move towards truth. Your teacher is always patient and kind so do not judge yourself. Go forward along your chosen path and find comfort and solace within the silence of your meditation. Face yourself, and be true to yourself, for you have to keep peace with your soul. Remember, your teacher is always willing to meet with you and impart knowledge, so strive to move closer and become at one with each other.

G Great will be your achievements as you accept love and truth as fundamental to living a full life. As you learn from experience and seek truth then your material and spiritual pathways will run parallel. As your pathways have two levels, one spiritual and the other material, so you become whole. Now you have truth and understanding of the natural laws and therefore you can pass on the knowledge that man strives to find. When you become whole and have gained knowledge and experience then you have fullness of life and nothing can destroy you, for death has no meaning and your horizon is limitless. You can only move closer to the Godhead and open your channel to serve God by allowing your gifts to be used by the spiritual forces that surround you. Harmony is yours forever so strive to keep the balance between your material and spiritual aspirations.

E Endurance. Your life is a test of endurance but with all your knowledge and understanding of the spiritual life you cannot fail. Be prepared to face adversity and do not run away from it. You must have strength to deal with all things and you must go forward with faith. For you have faith in yourself and faith in the Love of God, so always be positive in your approach and you will move forward in your quest for knowledge. As you face each stage of your physical life so your spirit responds to all the lessons you have learnt. Find contentment and peace as you walk your pathway and as you do so, so you will be able to help and encourage others to seek the truth. As you become a whole person so you will find that truth, love and peace, lead you forward to a greater understanding of the Godhead, the Divine Spirit.

25th August, 1987

Lightning Source UK Ltd.
Milton Keynes UK
174029UK00001B/63/P